A FLIP-THE-FLAP BOOK OF PREHISTORIC ANIMALS

DINOSAUR DINOSAUR

WRITTEN AND ILLUSTRATED BY

MATT COSGROVE

BACKPACKBOOKS
·
NEW YORK

Text copyright © 2004 by Matt Cosgrove
Illustrations copyright © 2004 by Matt Cosgrove
This 2006 edition published by Backpack Books, New York, NY,
by arrangement with Allied Publishing Group, Inc.
All rights reserved.
ISBN 0-7607-7061-1
Manufactured in China
06 07 08 09 10 MCH 10 9 8 7 6 5 4 3 2 1
First US edition published in 2005 by Flying Frog Publishing,
an imprint of Allied Publishing Group, Inc.

Dinosaur, dinosaur,
big
or small.

Are you short...

or are you

tall?

Dinosaur, dinosaur,
how do you roam?
In a group ...

or all alone?

Dinosaur, dinosaur,
on the go.

Are you

fast...

or are you slow?

Dinosaur, dinosaur,
where can you be?

High in the sky...

or deep
in the sea?

Dinosaur, dinosaur,
strong and tough.

Are you smOOth...

Dinosaur, dinosaur,
what do you eat?
Do you like plants...

or do you
like meat?

Dinosaur, dinosaur,
under attack.

Do you fight
from the front...

or from the back?

a mystery?